Earthquakes!
What Causes
Them?

by Stacey Sparks
illustrated by Stephen Nau

Scott Foresman

Editorial Offices: Glenview, Illinois • New York, New York
Sales Offices: Reading, Massachusetts • Duluth, Georgia
Glenview, Illinois • Carrollton, Texas • Menlo Park, California

Before   **After**

Think about the ground under your feet. It is solid. It is safe. It is still. The ground is all of these things—most of the time.

But sometimes, in some places, the ground shakes. This is called an earthquake.

Once every thirty seconds there is
a little earthquake somewhere in the
world. People may feel the earth move,
but nothing serious happens.

Every few months, there is a major
quake somewhere. Cracks open in the
ground. Buildings and bridges fall down.

Some earthquakes cause huge waves.
When these waves hit harbors, they can
pull boats off their anchors and toss them
onto the land.

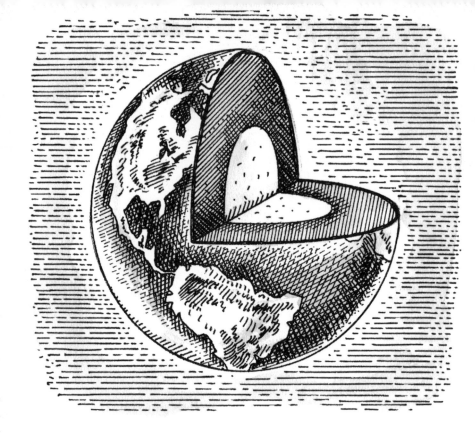

To understand earthquakes, it helps to know more about the Earth.

The Earth is made of three layers of rock. The top layer is the crust. It is between five and thirty miles thick. The next layer is the mantle. It is almost two thousand miles thick. The center of the Earth is called the core. It is over two thousand miles thick.

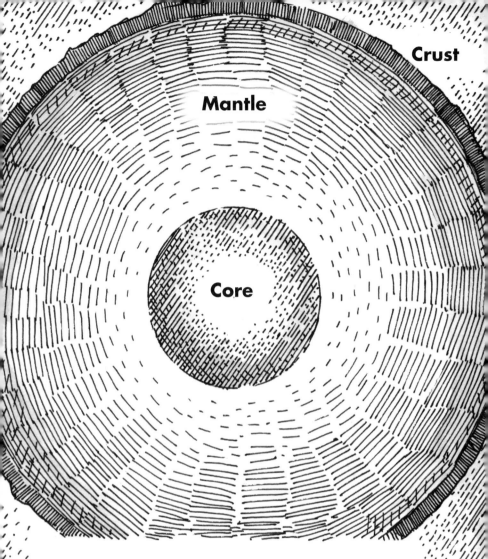

The core of the Earth is very hot. So is the mantle. Some of the rock in the mantle is so hot that it has melted. Just think of it! This rock is not hard like a pebble. It is soft, like paste.

Plate

The hot rock in the Earth's mantle is moving. It flows and bubbles, like boiling water in a pan.

The moving rock of the mantle pushes against the crust.

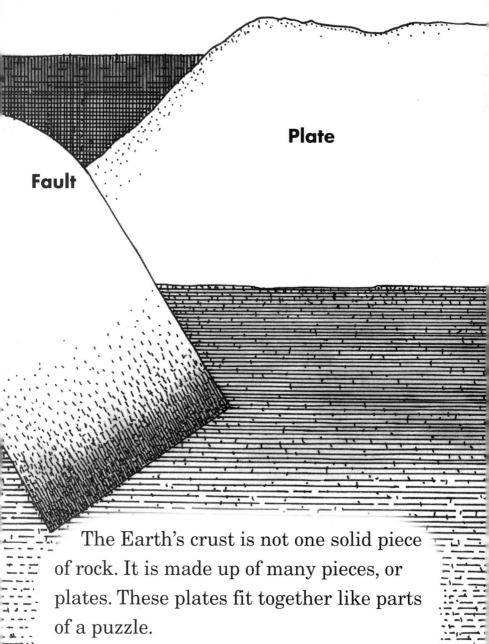

Plate

Fault

The Earth's crust is not one solid piece of rock. It is made up of many pieces, or plates. These plates fit together like parts of a puzzle.

The place where two parts of the crust meet is called a fault.

The Earth's Fault Lines

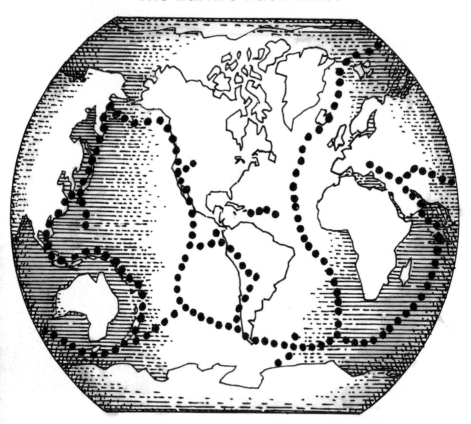

When melted rock pushes up against the plates, they move. Sometimes they slide smoothly, and no one feels anything. At other times, they bump hard against each other. Then the Earth shakes.

Most earthquakes happen along the Earth's fault lines.

California

San Francisco

San Francisco is one of the most beautiful cities in the world. But it is built over a fault. In 1906, the Earth shook along this fault. The earthquake almost destroyed this city.

It was the morning of April 18, 1906, and most people were still in bed.

A man awakened early to a scene that shocked him. The street was moving in waves. It looked as if the land had become the sea.

Houses began to vibrate and sway. Smokestacks toppled. Big buildings collapsed to the ground. Bells clanged. The earthquake continued for about one minute.

People fled from their houses. They looked around in shock and panic. Then they started to hear frantic calls for help. Some people were trapped under wrecked buildings.

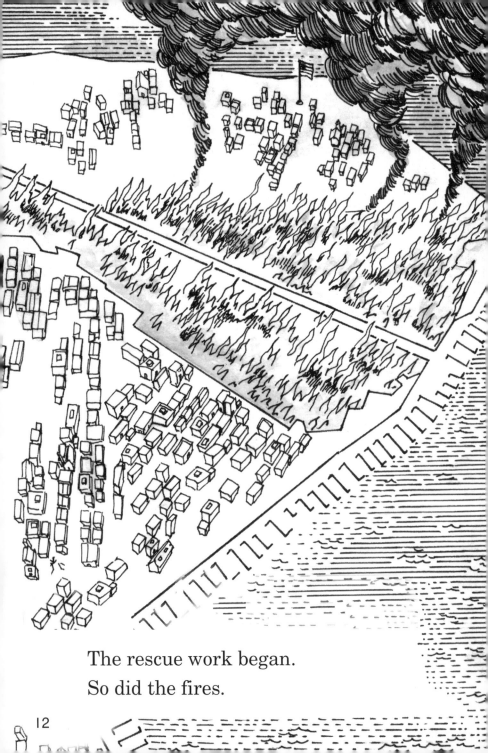

The rescue work began.
So did the fires.

Under the city streets, there were
pipes. Some carried water, while others
carried gas for lighting stoves and lamps.

The earthquake cracked many of the
gas pipes. Gas leaked into the streets.
Fires broke out.

Firefighters sped to put out the flames.
They turned on the hydrants and waited,
but no water gushed out.

The water pipes had cracked too.

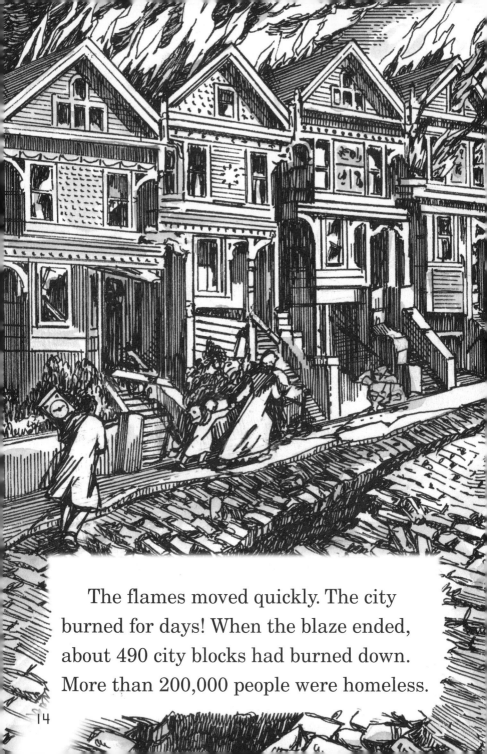

The flames moved quickly. The city burned for days! When the blaze ended, about 490 city blocks had burned down. More than 200,000 people were homeless.

Other areas have also been hit with strong earthquakes. In 1964, a big quake hit Alaska. The ground shook for nearly seven minutes. Cars bounced up and down. Houses split in two; streets opened up. When the quake was over, much of Alaska's coast had a new shape.

In 1923, a huge wave hit the coast of Japan. An earthquake under the sea caused this wave. Japan has about 1,500 earthquakes every year. Luckily, most of them are small.

Today, we have tools that can tell us when an earthquake is about to happen. These tools give people a chance to leave and find shelter somewhere else—until the Earth is still again.